Songs From Under the River
a collection of poetry

ᴄ◌

by Anis Mojgani

Write Bloody Publishing
America's Independent Press

Austin, TX

WRITEBLOODY.COM

Mojgani, Anis.
1ˢᵗ edition.
ISBN: 978-1938912-24-5

Interior Layout by Lea C. Deschenes
Cover Designed by Anis Mojgani & Joshua Grieve
Author Photo by Alexis Mojgani
Cover Illustration and Interior Illustrations by Anis Mojgani
Proofread by Alex Kryger
Edited by Alexis Mojgani, Cristin O'Keefe Aptowicz, and Derrick Brown
Type set in Bergamo from www.theleagueofmoveabletype.com

Printed in Tennessee, USA

Write Bloody Publishing
Austin, TX
Support Independent Presses
writebloody.com

To contact the author, send an email to writebloody@gmail.com

MADE IN THE USA

For Jean Gill
and her 5th period Creative Writing Class,
for Marc Smith and this amazing thing he began,
for those of you who listened over the years
and for you reading this.

And for AM, age 18,
falling in love with poetry.
I'm happy you did.

Do not weigh my eyes with pennies
—let me steal the heron's boat.
I will row upstream to the mouth of the river
to talk with the souls who gather there.
They will tell me songs of silver,
and I will sing them back to you.

SONGS FROM UNDER THE RIVER

LETTER TO THE READER

1995. New Orleans. The summer before I started college. I was reading an article about Poetry Slams. I had started writing poems earlier that year due to a creative writing class I took the last year of high school. The teacher, Ms. Gill, opened me up to what poetry could mean and to all the doors inside of me it could unlock. Reading about the slam opened more of those doors.

What I learned from the Slam is that poetry is not just for a small percentage of the population and that poetry shouldn't be dismissed by those who have never before connected to it. The Slam allowed for poetry that was written by anyone who had something in their heart to express and the willingness to share it. And it was judged by whoever had ears opened wide enough to listen and say, "Yes, that poem affected me," or, "No, that poem did nothing for me." There is a beautiful thing in allowing an audience to voice their love for or rejection of a piece of art, all while giving artists of all types, talents, and skill the space and time to share their own emotions and beliefs.

Many of the poems in this collection were written as I was first studying Slam and the poetry performed within it. They were written in college when I was exploring what it meant for me to write poetry with the desire to share my words aloud. I hesitate to use the term spoken word because I prefer the naming of a medium to the labeling of an instrumentation. I feel this would be similar to a musician who plays the banjo who when asked what he makes answers that he creates songs for the banjo rather than simply saying that he makes music.

I enjoyed making different kinds of art, and rather than narrowing my artistic outlets, I allowed anything inside me attempting to speak to find the appropriate medium by which to make itself heard. Sometimes that was through comics. Sometimes it was a painting. Sometimes it was a poem. And no matter what it was there was still different avenues within the medium itself. Some poems are content to sit in the wide expanse of a page. While some poems ripple their bodies slightly off the paper's surface and still others that breathe loudly behind your eyes and find their way to your throat.

One of the things I love about poetry that is performed or shared aloud is the ethereality of it. I love that a product of creativity, while existing in the same body with which it was born, may move in different cloaks. That the cloaks change based on where the artist is in the moment he or she opens his or her mouth. Or what the space is in which they are performing. Or the type of audience that is there to receive the work. The cloaks change due to the

sounds in the room, the light of the day, what he or she ate for dinner——
for an infinite number of reasons. And because of these changing cloaks, the
thing itself slightly changes. Thus every time it is shared, it becomes a unique
experience— not only for the audience but also for the artist and for the art
itself. While sharing the same space, an audience and an artist use the art to
engage in a conversation, the result of which is a completely new piece of
work, both original and singular to that moment in space and time. The art is
a ghost. A constant ghost, birthing and dying all the time.

It has been a long time since most of these poems had a place to rest their
bodies. When I was in college, I started self-publishing my work in poetry
chapbooks. I had been writing and performing my work regularly for a few
years at the open mics in the poetry community of Savannah, GA. My friend
Jon Reeves had been putting together chapbooks and suggested I put one
out. So with his help, I put out *Where Are You Moon?!* in 2001. Between then
and 2005, three more followed: *The Ballad of Nicor Misgoni, Untitled,* and *The
Birthday Yard.* A number of the these poems were used when I first began
competing in poetry slams and eventually became the backbones of my live
shows: "Shake the Dust" , "Galumpf deez nuts..." , "Direct Orders" , and
"The Pledge" , to name a few. There were other poems that never found
there way into those early chapbooks, such as "Here Am I" and my poem
about riding a bus and meeting a young boy named Quentin.

I have been writing poetry now for 18 years. Some poems have been not so
good, others pretty decent. Being 35 is very different than being 20 (or even
than being 25 or 30 for that matter). It's hard to remember when exactly, but
I wrote "Shake the Dust" at some point around 22 years old. It is probably
the most well-known and popular of my poems. It is one that seems to have
resonated with people back when I wrote it, and, thankfully, still seems to
resonate with people today. I created this piece when I was so much wetter
behind the ears, and I still ask, "Is this good? Does this work on a page?
Should this line be changed, this stanza cut? Does anyone even care about
reading the poetic rambling joyous frustration of a twenty-something college
kid?"

But I'm not sure how relevant it is to make the poetic sensibilities I had 15
years ago accountable to the ones I currently have.

We move through many orchards throughout our life. There are so many
orchards of so many trees, that we and those around us have planted. The
trees push through the earth to bear fruit. The earth is harder in some
place, softer in others. Some of the fruit blossoms in spring, some of it falls
in autumn. Some of the apples fall before they have sweetened, while with

some peaches you cannot stop the juice from running down your face. Some of the trees grow majestically, while others break before their time. There are so many trees and so many orchards. There are stories in all their trunks, hanging off every branch.   And for those who have found solace and shade from anything I might have planted, I thank you. I hope you enjoy.

—Anis Mojgani

CLOSER

Come closer.

Come into this. Come closer.

You are quite the beauty. If no one has ever told you this before know that right now. You are quite the beauty. There is joy in how your mouth dances with your teeth. Your mouth is a sign of how sacred your life truly is. So come into it. Come closer. Know that whatever God prays to, He asked it to help Him make something of worth. He woke from His dreams, scraped the soil from the spaces inside Himself, made you, and was happy. You make the Lord happy.

Come into this.

Come closer.

Know that something softer than us, but just as holy planted the pieces of Himself into our feet that we might one day dance our way back to Him. Know that you are almost home.

So come closer, come into this. There are birds beating their wings beneath your breastplate gentle sparrows aching to sing—come aching hearts! Come soldiers of joy, doormen of truth! Come true-of-heart.

Know this: my heart was too big for my body so I let it go. And most days, this world has thinned me to the point where I am just another cloud forgetting another flock of swans—having shaved off so many of my corners that I have felt at home only in the shape of a ball, bending myself so far backwards that the song of my mother believed I was returning I home. But believe me when I tell you my soul somehow still squeezes into narrow spaces. Place your hand beneath your head when you sleep tonight and you may find it there making beauty as we sleep, as we dream, as we turn over. When we turn over in the ground may the ghosts that we have asked answers of do the turning, kneading us into crumbs of light and into this thing-love-thing called life. Come into it.

Come, you wooden museums,
you gentle tigers.

Come, negro farces in two broken scenes.
Come, you rusting giants—

I see teacups in your smiles, upside down, glowing. Your hands are like my heart. Some days all they do is tremble. I am like you. I am like you. I too at times am filled with so much fear. But like a hallway, must find the strength to walk through it. Walk through this with me. Through this church that is ours— this church of bone, birthed of blood and muscle, where every move our arms make and every breath we swallow is worship. If we choke, it is only on songs. Bend with me. In this church of ours.

There is a doorknob glowing like chance. Clutch it. Turn and pull. Step through. Chin up. Back straight. Eyes open. Hearts loud.
Walk through this with me.
Walk through this with me.

ON THE DAY HIS SON WAS BORN
THE ASTRONOMER SCREAMED OUT HIS WINDOW

I found you inside a book of stars called
Sunday Starts at Saturday's Dusk.
It was turned to a page marked "For when."
I crumpled up my spine and became a mouse.
You were a planet.
I was the one prayer spoken
in the short little life of a dust mite
trying to be a sword
hoping to become a twig
a constellation
or at least an answer
to somebody's question.
I was born in the year of the swan.
My arms were born in the year of the fish.
My tongue felt like truth.
I had trouble swallowing it.
A corner of me was something truly spectacular.
My mother wrote the origins of myth
on the inside of my underpants.
I walked pantless to become closer to what I was.
I set the wheelbarrow on fire
climbed inside
and looked for a hill to ride down.
I was at the bottom of one.
I pushed the barrow up it.
Halfway up it rained.
Cussing doesn't come from a lack of vocabulary—
I know all the other words.
None of them speak the same language
that my fucking heart does.

Here Am I

We all wanted that high school sweetheart.
We wanted to be young in the fifties
with meatloafs and sock hops
and lawns so perfect
they looked like Clark Gable was kissing them.

We wanted to be thirteen and alive
and meet a girl that was thirteen and alive.
To walk with her past the grandstands.
To sit and hold hands with, to sit and talk with,
to sit and kiss with, to sit and sit with
like this was something you lost and found.
But that never was.

We once wanted to be poor but not too poor.
To connect this country like Kerouac and thumbs
pulling small town waitresses
into back seats and trailer parks homes
where the two of you would find passion expanding
between the locking of your bones
until morning would come to find you out on the road
with your pockets empty except for your hands.
But your hands would be overflowing with your soul.
But that's not what happened.

We once climbed into bed as though between the sheets
was a valley where dinosaurs still lived.
And how we would explore them with a flashlight
catching these triceratops and brontosauruses.
But even he was opened with the dripping teeth of reality.
With the smoke that rose out of the homes
on the corners we once climbed through—
the streets and footballs with which we once threw—
the school desks upon which we once drew—
the windows that sat open,
through which we once flew.
And the outside world of parking spaces and dead friends
came flooding on in, and we forgot what we wanted
and became what we become.
Waitresses and bartenders.

City employees and temp positions.
We are junkies and one-kiss poems
and we cry the stars.

As we write our scars
on dumpsters and electric boxes—
because the only thing we can hear is our hearts
and the streets are the only ones listening
to this blood that breathes through the letters we leave.
We dream to rise out of these burning buildings,
but instead we get buried somewhere beneath them.
Because I know my life is like some high school kid's notebook—
that kid who goes back and forth between school and home,
stacking the letters and the pictures too close
for anyone outside of his own imagination to read
because it's through the ink that his heart beats,
that his heart breathes—
and we all wanted to pass these notes—
check if you like me
check if you don't
check if you'll date me
check if you won't.
Because we all wanted the love songs to be true.

And we all once loved dinosaurs.

And we wanted the stars to hold our hands—
to lick the teeth
to fuck us
but they ended up fucking us.

So let your smiles twist.
Like my heart dancing precariously
on the edge of my finger tips,
staining them like that same high school kid
licking his thoughts using his sharpie tip
writing, "I was here."
I was here, motherfucker.
And ain't none of y'all can write that
in the spot that I just wrote it in.
I am here motherfucker
and we all here motherfucker
and we all motherfuckers motherfucker.

Because every breath I breathe brings me closer
to the day when my mother will die.
And every breath I take
takes me a second further
from the moment she caught my father's eye.
And every word I carry
is another stone to put into place
in the foundation I'm building to ease the days
and help erase something I never saw—
what all of us wanted and what none of us got—
what we all had and have and what we all forgot—
that we all wanted to be something—
that we all became something.
And it may not be what we once thought it would be,
but something is still something
and like some cats say,
something's better than nothing.
Feet are smarter than an engine,
and dreams are stronger than thighs.
And questions are the only answers we need
to know that we are as alive
as a time when I held the mind of a child asking:
Why is 2 + 3 always equal to 5?
Where do people go when they die?
What made the beauty of the moon—
the beauty of the sea?
Did that beauty make you?
Did that beauty make me?
Will it make me
something?

Will I be something?

Am I something?

And the answer comes:

You already are.

You always were.

And you still have time to be.

I Sing a Song of Jacob

We used to swim in your river together and jump into it from the big branches of the thick trees above. A month ago, your mother Kate found you lying on the floor. Your heart had stopped and she tried to beat it back to life.

We would play football in the street, throw rubber balls against the marble walls of office buildings, catching them in our nine-year-old hands. You moved from New Orleans, an hour away, to the country. Thirty acres named Dayspring. On Saturdays, we would drive there and feel the presence of God napping amongst the trees.

That weekend I spent at your house, I remember your father George brought home pastries from the city and that you and I chopped fresh strawberries from the garden, stirred them into the last bit of vanilla ice cream in the freezer. It is still the best strawberry ice cream I have ever had.

You were always so *shai-tu-nack*—the naughty one. We talked of how Jacob loved to use the words "turd" and "crap." No one could play Double Dribble on Nintendo like you could—when your players would pass the ball, it was just a blur with sound. You grew tall enough to dunk on the goal out back and your face reminded people of John Cusack's. On the volleyball court we'd joke about slamming the ball down each other's puny throats. In your attic bedroom we danced to rap, swung our arms under the black light and glow in the dark stars. You drew muscle men, showed me paintings of New York, and I grew up with you.

You were 16 years of my life.

I think of the tree we found in the woods that we had planned to turn into a secret cave. I think of ghost stories and flashlights, the rope swing. Summers and the movies and the hugs. I think of the tattoos you drew for others, the ones that decorated your limbs, the comics we would dream, and the stars we could see from your porch. Of the three-year-old daughter Chloe that you left and of your beautiful parents, your brother, your two sisters, and of how I saw everyone but you this past July in Milwaukee. I saw everyone but you because you were back home working. And I asked George how you were, and he told me that things were good, that you were getting yourself back together, that your days were coming back around.

My father told me, at your funeral, you were buried at home. And before the coffin was laid beneath, your graffiti friends spray painted and marked it for you. And afterwards everyone played volleyball.

Let this page be the casket in which my memory of you floats and these words my tag for you, scrawling my love for my brother Jacob Simmons, as God brushes the hair from your brow now, collecting your sweat to pour on the earth from the heavens, into the wet nights of children dreaming. And may they grow like you did: in your own way, but always up.

For Those Who Can Still Ride an Airplane For the First Time

I'm 35 years old and am still trying to figure out
what being a man means.
I don't drink fight or love,
but these days I find myself wanting to do all three.
And I don't really have a favorite color anymore,
but I did when I was a kid.
And back then that color was blue.
And back then I wanted to be an architect
an artist
an astronaut
a secret agent
a ranger for the World Wildlife Fund
and a hobo.
And when I was six years old, I used to throw my clothes
into my blue-and-yellow plastic-and-vinyl
Hot Wheels car-carrying suitcase and run away
to beneath the dining room table.

I've made out with more girls than I wish I had
and not nearly as many as I would like to.
I've been in love 4 or 5 times,
so I doubt I'm gonna try that much more often.
And I spend most days making pictures
or thinking about making pictures.
Or masturbating or thinking about masturbating.
And I dream too much
and I don't write enough
and I'm trying to find God everywhere.
In this world of fast faces, I'm trying
to figure out this thing He made called a man.

And the television tells me that it's bare-knuckled bombing.
And if I had a tank or was a movie star,
my penis would be huge
because that's what they keep telling me.
And that's what I want
because that's what being a man means,
or at least that's what they keep telling me.

My Pops. He takes care of us.
He puts the garbage out twice a week.
He drives forty-five minutes to water flowers.

I'm sitting on a bus
when a seven-year-old boy carrying a book of Robin Hood
sits down next to me and asks me my name.
Anis.
That's a nice name.
Thank you, what's yours?
Quentin.
Anis? Do you wanna read with me?

So tell me what my fists keep writing.

My fingers open like gates when I type,
and the wind is swinging in the wake.
I lift bridges with poems, and forests grow
in my mother's eyes.
I am looking for God, Quentin,
while this world forgets you for trying.
For this world hates your eyes Quentin.
For they are simple and they are pure.
And Quentin, this world hates your fingers—
little like the stems of flowers—
for not being able to pick up the things you have left behind—
simply because you are still learning to do so.
I don't drink fight or fuck, but these days, Quentin,
it's only two out of those three that I don't do.
And I've fallen in love 6 7 8 9 10 times, Quentin,
so I don't want to want to but I still do.
And I want to find God in the morning—
and in the tired hands of dusk
at the mouth of the river
and down by its feet—
but instead, I drive sixty
through residential streets
praying to hit a child
that he may stay forever full of night,
with simple outstretched limbs
trying to pick up way too much way too fast,
forgetting what it means
to be a person in a world

where egos are measured with tabloids.
Where automobiles double for morals.
Where beliefs are like naps—
you leave them behind when somebody touches you.
And in a place where oil somehow
always takes precedence over life.
I find myself sitting on a bus
watching a small boy float down like fresh water,
carrying a book I used to carry,
asking if I want to share what he sees—
if only for a little while, and I do.

And then asks if I want to give to him what I see—
if only for a little while.
And I read to him.
And then says to me he is going to show me the world
and starts reading me the sentences himself,
his hands dancing back and forth, stumbling
over words, not noticing
all the time
what is written,
sometimes skipping whole lines
because his fingers are moving
faster than what they are showing his eyes
and I want to tell him slow down, Quentin.

Slow down, Quentin.

You don't have to touch and go.
You can see it all if your finger whispers on one word.
Slow down, and hold what you see just a little while longer.

For in a world full of fast faces,
I'm looking for God everywhere—
trying to figure out a little better
this little thing He made called a man.

CHURCH

In the broken comma of dawn,
I become my father.

Hope can be a dirty word
and even dirtier when one forgets to use it.

I once maybe wanted a house.
A red, wooden one.

With a fence
a hill
a wife

two children

maybe three
maybe one

a stack of breaths
to pull and turn through

and a God
that took me in
and kept me warm.

Peacocks

He reads a letter out loud and cannot do so without stopping. His round arms tremble. You can see there are tears being pushed down. The arms straighten. His son watches him. He reads on, about martyrs in Iran dying, their numbers increasing day to day.

He came to Louisiana when he was 19 years old to learn how to apply his slide rule and his ears. When asked if he dreams in English or Farsi he says sometimes both. He has not smelled Tehran in 42 years. He was not there when the Revolution dragged bodies with brick and fire and buried women dressed in ash.

The man's son wonders if his father feels like he ran from something, wonders if his father works as hard as he does as a self-imposed penance for that feeling, pushing the shovel to build prayers that stand like shrines. The man swings his voice and stands to the East every day speaking to God, asking for his lord to shape him into something shaped a bit more like the slow, glow shoulders of these drained souls.

There are shahs and priests that still scream and weep outside of paradise for the skulls they skinned— for the piles they made of hair and beliefs, peeled back and scraped bare from bones. His skull is still here. Skin peeking through the thin, soft black hair that he has passed onto his two oldest. He works harder than ghosts to keep his heart in this world and his hands in the other, touching doors when no one is looking, searching for poems he buried inside the mother of his children. He sees the pages writing themselves in their faces. He tries not to stare too long, too hard. He may see too much of himself. The birds he was. Carrying islands in their beaks, clutching Persia in their wings, painting their feathers in watermelon juice. He drinks salt. Sleeps with his throat open. And waits for these gentle sparrows to fly back inside his mouth, carrying into him the cries of those Persians that no one will know taste or ever hear of. Hymns of what he is. Whispers of where he comes from. The gentle memory-limbs of his cousins and aunts. Those pillars of poetry and beauty that held up Shiraz, city of mighty domes that cut stars down and named them, before melting that silver down into petty bullets and thin wires to tighten like knuckles around throats that stood thick like prayers, spines standing straight as rifles, offering the echoes of themselves into the heavens.

Most nights he stays up until he dreams by accident, his computer in his lap, falling asleep on the couch.

His sons ride on gray and black stringed wolves. They beat their drums until their legs vibrate open, carrying souls shaped like the shells of an elephant gun, wondering how to be more. Wondering how to curve arms into a cradle instead of a coffin. How to hold their father's brow to their hearts as though the beating inside them were the soft warble of the river's current. May his sons pray that when he goes the angels trawl his veins for the pearls that swim inside of them, pulling them to the surface, that God may swallow them softly. Carrying them back down into the precious source that they came out from and holding him in the mighty water like a whispering psalm, emptying his rooms, his hands, his shoulders, and rocking him gently to sleep.

21 Thoughts on the Stereotype that All Brown People Are Terrorists

1. My mother is Black. My father Iranian. As an American, this means I am born under two bad signs.

2. Acts of terror are constituted by the use of violence against civilians to intimidate and induce fear for political, religious, or other ends.

3. I am not certain, but I do not think every brown thing is hoping to commit acts of terror. I have encountered a number of brown dogs that were not terrorists. This is not to equate the brown man with a dog. I'm just saying—it's interesting.

4. I have known my fair share of white dogs that were total shits.

5. My parents have three brown chairs. Only one of them is a terrorist. Even this cannot be proven.

6. Mount Rushmore. Not a terrorist.

7. Do you remember the craziness that came with the sorrow of this country after 9/11? How crazed we were with fear? I had dreams of men on the street beating my father to death because of his name and accent.

8. My father. Not a terrorist.

9. The census labels Middle Eastern as Caucasian.

10. Dick Cheney. Not brown.

11. Noam Chomsky says, "If they do it, it's terrorism. If we do it, it's counter-terrorism." The machine of propaganda is a strange and colorblind and colorful machine. During World War II, comic books pushed forward stories centered around American supermen triumphing over the evil Germans and Japanese. It is always easiest to turn our hearts by affecting our eyes.

12. The Red Scare was based on fear of the unknown. Fear of opposing ideologies. McCarthyism was a terrorist act committed by a government on its own people.

13. Ten years after the buildings fall, I am in the airport security line and the woman asks me if my name, sounding a tad bit foreign, and my face, looking a tad bit Baghdad, asks if the name is a family name. I have never known there to be a different kind.

14. Growing up, my favorite show was *MacGyver*. For those of you unfamiliar with it, *MacGyver* dealt with a gentleman who could make explosives out of whatever happened to be on hand, be it a peppermint and a ball of string, or a pencil case and three cardboard tubes. I watched it religiously for years. I never learned how to make a bomb from watching it. Perhaps this was not the case with other brown people.

15. Osama Bin Laden. Not white.

16. My friend Tim Perkins told me when he was a kid he went to a largely black school. He's white. One day, his friends were talking about white folks and he asked "Well, what about me?" They said, "You're not white. You're Italian." This has nothing to do with terrorists. I just find it interesting.

17. The most famous American domestic terrorist, Timothy McVeigh, killed 168 innocent people in the Oklahoma City Bombing. Timothy McVeigh. Not Italian.

18. The IRA has committed acts of terror for 70+ years. Britain began theirs long before this.

19. The American presidency, like the leadership of all nations, comes with it the administrating of acts of terror for the betterment and protection of its citizens. The terrorist acts from our leaders that we do not hear of do not mean these presidents were more courageous and didn't commit terrorism. Only that they were quieter.

20. Sometimes when I watch television I ask myself, "Is that brown man a terrorist? What about that one? And that one, is he?" The first man is Wayne Brady. Obviously. The second is Aziz Ansari. The third is my President. I do not know the answers to my questions.

21. Public Enemy tells me this country has a fear of a black planet. Such heavy clothing fear becomes upon our bodies. Your coat will not protect you, no matter how clean, how starched, how bright, how white it may be. We are all Russians. Every one of us Russians, born under a strange time in American history.

AUTOBIOGRAPHY

I share a birthday with ice cream
asteroid #132 Aethra
and the ticker-tape parade
for Charles Lindbergh's homecoming.

DIRECT ORDERS

You have been given a direct order to rock the fuck out.

Rock out like you were just given the last rock 'n' roll record on earth and its minutes are counting down the moments to flames.

Rock out like you just won both Showcase Showdowns.

Rock out like the streets are empty except for you, your bicycle, and your headphones.

Rock out like your lips were just placed on a break-dancing muse with legs that go all the way up.

Rock out like Publisher's Clearing House is ringing your front door.

Rock out like you'll never have to open up a textbook again.

Rock out like you get paid to disturb the peace.

Rock out like music is all that you got.

Rock out like you were standing on a rooftop and the city is as loud and glowing as a river flowing below you.

Rock out like the plane is going down and there are 120 people onboard and 121 parachutes.

Rock out like the streets and the books are all on fire and the flames can only be extinguished by doing the Electric Slide.

Rock out like it's Saturday afternoon and Monday is a national holiday.

Rock out like somebody's got a barrel pointed to your temple saying Rock out like your life depended on it fool!
because it does.

Rock out like your eyes are fading but you still got your ears but you don't know for how long so rock out like 5 o'clock time
meant pop 'n' lock time.

Rock out like you've got a pair of pants full of tokens and nothing to do but everything.

Rock out like you are the international Skee-ball champion of the entire universe.

Rock out like you just escaped an evil orphanage to join a Russian circus.

Rock out like your hero is fallen and you are spinning your limbs until they burst into a flaming pyre of remembrance.

Rock out like you are enslaved in the South and dancing
is all that you have to know who you are.

Rock out like your dead grandfather just came back to take a ride with you in your brand new car.

Rock out like the table was full.

Rock out like the neighbors are away.

Rock out like the walls won't fall but dammit you're gonna die trying to make them.

Rock out like the stereo's volume knob only has the figure 8
of infinity on it instead of merely numbers.

Rock out like it's raining outside and you got a girl to run through it with.

Rock out like you were playing football in the mud and your washing machine ain't broken.

Rock out like you threw your window open on your honeymoon because you want the whole world to know what love is.

Rock out like you just got a book published.

Rock out like you just went to your high school reunion to find out everyone, even the women, are all ugly and balding except for the former captain of the cheerleaders who has just been divorced by her impotent husband and she only has eyes for you.

Rock out like you've got a date with Heidi Klum.

Rock out like the shadow of man passes behind you, drops you to your knees, you're buckling in a sweat, cold metal is pressed to the back of your skull, the trigger is pulled, and the gun jams.

Rock out like you got an empty appointment book and a full tank of gas.

Rock out like Jimi has returned carrying brand new guitar strings.

Rock out like the mangos are in season.

Rock out like the record player won't skip.

Rock out like this was the last weekend,
like these were the last words,
like you don't ever want to forget how.

Parade Day

confetti and graffiti give me the same feeling
that something won or someone came home from far far away
there are days when I am surprised that the streets
are not run rampant with both
that there is not kissing in the streets
that there is not the rock song everlasting of fireworks explosion
that the streets are not overflowing
with slow-driving convertible parades
and beautiful queens
waving at us
there are some hours where I am surprised
that there is no parade scheduled
simply because we all woke up and did it—
we were human!
today!
we were human!
yesterday! we were the same thing
and tomorrow—
again!

filled with blue mountain lust and skyscraper
we are skyscrapers
we are whatever is bigger than skyscrapers

broken balls of gas and matter that have traveled far
from whatever corner spat them out
into the contraction and expansion of space
that is the same pulse of the forest
sections of this universe that moved through space
until it found something soft to move through
bits of paper broken and torn
from larger sheets
curved and curling in the wind

sign your name across my back
it is not the concrete poured into the foundation
that makes the buildings able to stand everyday
but rather the words burned across their faces and feet

that some stranger loved them
or loved themselves enough to do that
sign your name across my back

it ain't the cinder in the timber
but the initials carved that break the trunk open
the tree flaunting its body
saying
look at me
look at what I got
somebody loved something hard enough to use a knife
look at what I got

WASHINGTON HEIGHTS

She would often take her time coming to bed.
The chemicals in her body hidden too high for me to see.
I would make the hours-long trek from Sunset Park
to that always-too-dark-to-breathe apartment
up in Washington Heights. It had wooden floors
and a long hallway you walked through
to get to the enormous living room.
She loved leopard print and the Beach Boys.
She would play me their records.
Her roommate talked a lot about Brian Wilson
and was almost out of his mind.
Wanting to be alone with her, I would retire early,
would lie there waiting for her to join me.
Trying to fall asleep, to not slowly drip through the boredom,
hoping she would save me from that,
wishing only to be close to her skin.
She would often stay up
getting high in her roommate's room.
When she came to bed we would stay up talking.
No matter how late it was, she always wanted
to fall asleep before the sun rose.
Said she couldn't stand being awake
long enough for its rays to show up.
To block out any early believers,
we slept with heavy drapes on the dirty windows.
During the night, the steam inside the radiator
would sometimes clink like some kind of ghost
swaying its chains in the same spot,
the sound rattling down the hall.
I caught long trains that winter.
Trudged through the cold
in my crummy boots to get there.
I would climb to the top of the stairs.
The building's floors covered in tiny white tiles.
She would open the black door of her home
with a big smile and hold me
with all her little body—
how soft,
how warm—

before taking my coat and socks,
wet with snow,
to lay them on top of the radiator,
leaving puddles on the hard wood
as we walked to the back of the apartment.
What a mansion we built between us.

DRAYTON STREET

Laying on our sides,
her hips like a soup spoon,
she told me,
"When you kiss me
my legs tickle."

from YOU ARE THE SEA

you are the sea
you are the coast
the rivers passing between
you sing synonymous with the universe
the view of Mars unnamed in another century
the fountain of revelation sprouting from the brow
sputtering the stutters of mechanical gods
the belt of Olympus
the color of magic things
the rainbows look at your dreams to remind them of home
they use the hills & valleys of your body as a postcard
you are the sweet songs children sing
whispering themselves to sleep
people call you the wind
people watch how you love the fields
people look up & write poems in the night about you
calling them The Moon
& The Constellations Carry a Big Stick When They Walk
I call you love
trace your maps & lines
the mountains that leak over
the rivers passing between
your holy coastline
you float inside the atmosphere of my arms
you are the sea
the shells on the beach I lift to my ear
they spell out your name your kiss
I hold on to my lips imagine they are yours
put shells stones and pebbles in my pocket
& feel your warmth upon my thigh
replace you for my femur
& I can walk again

In My Library There Are 17 Books

1

I wore a shrine to you above my head for so many years.
It sparkled like a Hindu god
and hung there
the heaviest of my heaviest hats.

2

My face it is a bicycle riding downhill.
Lick me with your headlights
I will forget my helmet at home
break my femurs upon your front fender.

3

I am filled with so much hip hop
my elbow rhymes with dirty sandwich.

4

My dirty sandwiched beatboxed
and my elbow said back:
I place two pancakes upon two plates
when I cut them back and forth the porcelain breaks.

5

I was never a broken man
but I too know how to pick the pieces up.
Some days the pieces are all teeth
pulled from the mouths of children.
Some days they are simply books
searching for a shelf.

6

I have carved shelves out of my heart
to try and bring an order to things.
All it did was make space.

7
The floor of my bedroom is a junkyard.
It is filled with the myth of a giant earth-sized snake.
Some days I am a god of thunder lifting cats.
Some days I walk nine paces
turn and fall over and over again.
I die every single time.

8
I know that peace can come with a popsicle stick
and that some ceilings are prayers to mustangs.
Staring into the chandelier's candles
I have begged for its heat to carry me out of some of these rooms
saw the eyebrows of God in furniture.

9
Some furniture looks at you disappointingly.
Some chairs still stare like they are still proud of what you are.

10
Some ladies' legs are shaped like confessionals
and some confessionals are built like the bows of burning boats.
Speaking through both my body caught fire like everything else.

11
I have devoured so many forests.
There is so much cedar wood in my belly.
So much sawdust on the floor of my love.
I have been sweeping it up for so many days of my life
but each day I sweep up a little bit more.
One day my floors will be clean.

12
I clench my hands into fists in case I run into myself.
I have something I want to give him.
I won't know what it is until he is standing before me
peeling open my hands.

13
I was eight years old
the first time I learned to breakdance
on the floor of Angela's bohemian loft.
Little Ray taught me the centipede.

He was 13 and had a skateboard
Was a lighthouse
a tower
Antarctica.
So damn cold he dropped the d
and came up with an extra o.

14
I have pulled the bones out of my body
and carved temples from them.
Look under my nails
there is holy text in there.
I do not know what it says
but some hours are spent
doing nothing but staring at the tips of my fingers.

15
Hold a mirror up to what I once was
you would see only guitar strings
shimmering in the light.

16
When I snaked my body like the river
I didn't even need the music to play.
The adults were in the other room.
I used the floorboards as the beat.
I stood up
dirt on my shirt
my teeth had been replaced with bits of gold.
An old man held me in a pan
ran water over my bones.
And from under the dirt of his palms
how I shone.
O how I shone.

THE MOON WAS A BACKYARD

We were hands making fists
around fistfuls of black hair
fistfuls so thick they were bushels
hair so black the night looked small
and hands clenched
so tightly
that God Himself could see
we all were scared
and blind
and little

LOVE IS NOT A SCIENCE

The bedroom is a morgue
The bed a slot car race

Memories are a rock
thrown through the window of an empty house

Love is a shirt you still wear
that has already stopped fitting

Flowers all have names—
the same names

The moon is a son of a bitch
The sun a mean mean star

The stars are tombstones
The constellations a graveyard

The flowers reach past their bones
to lay themselves across the feet of dead animals

The dead animal is a quiet sadness
a quiet cross made over the chest

A prayer is a quiet kiss
given to the solar system

A rooftop is a telephone to heaven
A telephone call has the sound of dirt

filling the grave back up
A conversation is a knife fight

The heart a flat tire
The Northwest was once a lighthouse

a joyous shout
now a stain

Portland is a deep hole I am trying to dig my way out of
The city of Eugene is a conman who stole my shovel

Ireland is a thief
Los Angeles a lie

New Orleans is a sad sad porch
it carries the baskets of slanted truths

The past is littered with No Trespassing signs
Writing poetry is drinking from a broken bottle

Memories are a broken vase
whose shape everyone remembers differently

I remember it having flowers—
a box for holding its petals

Flowers all have one name
Goodbye is a pocketknife that doesn't close properly

Goodnight is an echo
Sleep sweetly an emptied rabbit hutch

The blanket replaces people
A teacup is too small a replacement

People replace a lover
Sleep is a battlefield

God takes naps
He dreams of the people who have left Him behind

Animals are saints—
learning to touch them brings one closer to that which was holy

The unicorn is not a lie the unicorn is real
I've seen it—its skin is blue, not white

Dance is a magic trick she rarely showed me
All I ever wanted was to see up her sleeves

The wrist is a lifeboat
The memory is death dressed in sanctuary

Oregon is a garden
All the flowers have the same name

They all grow
in the direction of her mother's house

Her hand holding mine
is a war I am afraid of losing

Hope is a blindfold
Thighs are a safehouse

The embrace is bathwater
The backbone a song

The body is Buddha singing it
The ear Krishna eating an apple behind it

The neck a monastery
A kiss the rosary

The mouth, an orchard
Her teeth sweet cherries

The words she says when sleeping are church
I would follow them over any mountain

Her voice is a big smile of a man who knows the way to go
Her voice is a big man I would follow over any mountain

Her voice is a mitten
Her voice is too far away

It is made up of air and vibrations
I do not know how to put my hands inside this kind of science

Every day
I pull on this coat of knives—

just try and hold me
Just try to hold me

SPILLING APPLES

When next she comes to kiss you, wrap yourself
in white paper. Like dead fish. Like the smell of the sea.
Sleep on crushed ice. Spill apples. Do not dream of orchards.
Throw blue and white bowls to the bright floor. Walk barefoot
over the tiles. Paint them red with your skin. The inside of you
is a big country. Gypsy your chest. Caravan it across. Sharpen
your suitcase. Knife the night. Watch as it bleeds. Fill the gutters
with meteorite hearts. Use their cold beauty to keep your organs
from turning. Sleep on crushed ice.

When she comes to kiss you, wrap yourself in white paper or
white sheets and pull her close to stain whatever you imagined
was the thing still keeping you clean. Crash your body over hers.
Seastorm your wrists. Shipwreck your intentions. Shipwreck
your past. The future has wet and dry sand. Make your bed in it.
Clutch the memory with both hands. Push it over her chest.
Rub it until it dissolves. Find the holes. Badger your hands
under her skin. The bumps on her heart
will language themselves.

OVER THE ANVIL WE STRETCH

At the head of the driveway was the banana tree.
At the foot of the drive was a black river I swam through.
Over the antique trunk in the living room
I remember my hands clasped,
praying out loud.

I remember our two screen doors.

I remember catching the salamander.

Standing in the forbidden broken shed
watching the old hay dying under the cracks of the sun.

The dead rat behind the bookstore
and the maggots moving through its purple skull.

Under the house
the tan dirt filling my lungs like the ash of bodies.

The lizard and how bright
how green he was.
So bright, his skin was almost an emerald fire.

Halfway through this city,
I sit with the back of a chair edged under the doorknob—
trying to cut my skull out with butterknives
trying to fly south, my flocks of thoughts
shooting down blackbirds with biscuits
throwing hard bread at the heads, trying to break their necks.
Get out of here, I say out loud.
The ghosts lay in the next room,
giggling in their sleep.
When they are awake
they ask for me by name.
They hold up their shining wrists.
The smell of the magnolia.
The trays of donuts at Pee-Wee's funeral.
Bicycles in the Marigny.
What necklaces they wear.

Every night is a struggle
to paint a grave on the back of my eyelids.
I keep cutting the roads off at the ankles,
cutting my legs off at the vein.
On the other side of the door
everyone waits for it—
for the sugar in my arms.
They want to taste my flesh.
I know that while they eat
they will hold me,
so I keep walking towards them.
My heart is big and clumsy.
All night long I scratch my face
until the mirrors become paintings of strangers.
Balancing an armful of bricks
I am learning to forget myself.

THE FISHERMAN

The fisherman throws his nets.
At night when he eats, he sits alone,
his plate round as the moon.
He lights one candle on the table
and peels the skin of his fish with his fork and knife,
peeling it back like a bedsheet.
Most days he wakes before the sun,
for the fish they do not sleep long.
Sometimes when he has been drinking heavily
he goes down to the rocks at night and he reads to the fish.
He reads to them poems.
Poems from books.
Poems about the human condition.
Poems about the muscles inside him that question and quiver
and shiver and sleep,
bottle in one hand
book in the other
—books clutching poems like they were their mothers—
too afraid to let their children out
into the soft fear of the electric night—
and he was the wild one to show them this world.
His mother will never hold him like that again he thinks—
I am too big.
Book in one hand
bottle in the other,
he reads the poems out loud,
spitting the words out like they were teeth he no longer needed
while the storms gather around him
like a flock of ballooned corpses.
He screams the poems
like a drunk preacher cutting a rope.
He slurs the screams—
picking up poems like stones
hurling them at the foot of God's throne
hurling word after word after word
waiting for some door in some black cloud to open up—
but nothing happens.
The rain falls. The waves swing.

The fish sleep
and wake
and sleep
and awaken again and again
in the rocking of the ocean.
He stands above them like Noah,
surrounded by bucket after overflowing bucket,
and all he has left to catch this wet lightning is this open mouth.
So he reads to them—
he reads to them about things none of them will ever see.
About flowers opening.
About birds large as cliffs—
holding heroes between their silver feathers,
carrying these warriors into the open grace of the gods,
and into a mighty providence that this fisherman stands inside of,
their shields and shoulders polished hard enough
to blind the sun right back.
He empties himself.
And the waves they swing.
He goes home and falls into bed.
Sleeps all the next day.
Night comes through his window like a fever
like a dream
like a mother holding him close.
He wakes wet inside her arms
goes to his kitchen
lights his candle
cooks his audience
and peels back its skin like a bedsheet
before crawling inside.

Galumpf Deez Nuts...
Galumpf Deez Nuts Spines Shoulders
& Collarbones Of Mine

In my underwear I write poetry
two headed poetry
three legged poetry
poetry with ten spigots and no training wheels
there are gold flames airbrushed across my back and I have bare feet
I have BEAR feet
RAAAARRRRHHHHHHGGGGGGGGGGGGGGGGHHH feet

speak up
I walk with big sticks in my ear
and am filling twigs with sentences
filing my nails down with memories
my love can shave diamonds
scientists speculate over it
I come from the moon
Neil and Buzz
and that third guy walked across my tummy
I giggled
and a spoonful of cherub tasted like cherries and wallabies
I write two underweared poems
my poems take off both underwears
and dance naked around the candelabra in the living room
I am writing wrists and rubberbands on the back of the belly's bathtub
pressing my lips to the shower's belly button
I whisper
the goat man is in the woods dancing
the golden nugget!
the chupacabra!
the book man!
there is a cloud splintering like a kneecap inside my leg
buy me pants mother
buy me a hat!
there are moths in my shoulders
I am shaking
I am full of love
I was full of love

I carved out pear shaped slices of it
and fed a million tired ankles
God sat on my shoulder like a cricket
I swatted a bee like a father's advice
and asked for it again
tell me where I can go
when every bridge has wheels running alongside its bottom
I write poems with no training wheels
I write my skull
like it was a color
I was picking up and examining inside my hands
for the very first time

at the corner of Central Park East and 63rd Street
I clutch an imaginary football like a small child
stand two inches in front of a yellow wall
and scream directly into the wall's bricks
GO DEEP!
and as I fling the pigskin forward I try to catch my childhood
bouncing back at me
GO DEEE E E P
!!

I AM A 3 HEADED GALUMPF
A BLUE GIRAFFE

A WATER FOUNTAIN ON THE MOON!!!

catch me carbon!
catch me galumpf!
catch me galumpf catcher
catch me Lord
hold me
like a bowl
like how the clouds
hold the moon
holding the rooftops of this city
holding me and mine and my memories
in my veins

there is a lonely mermaid
murmuring
all
day
long

she singy sing sings
such
beeauuu
tiful
songs

her throat
is a girl I once knew

her nose it is made of silver
her backbone is a plum

her backbone
is a plum

& Then Billy Explained to Me the Parts of the Gun

1
Have her hold you how the holster holds the hip,
carrying so close to your hands
something to protect yourself.

2
Hold me how the holster holds the hip.
Carrying so close to my hands
something to protect myself.

In some songs
this body of mine still beats like a drum for yours.

3
Our skin was shed from the same single grass blade.

4
The footsteps taken inside of me,
they run fast and echo long and loud.
I hear the floorboards in that house
creak still
under my feet,
and sometimes it is all I can do
to sit quietly in the middle of that cacophony.

5
In the summer nights
I open the windows and stare at the sky.
I can smell the jasmine on its wrists.

6
The gun's caliber is .44,
its handle inlaid with pearl.
When I hold it
my hand
sometimes trembles.
But every empty can on that fence

I hit
dead center in their labels.
I can hear the wind whistling
through them holes.
And all them shadows
whistle their way on as well.

THE BALLAD OF NICOR MISGONI

I like my eggs scrambled
because I prefer function over form

When I drive I shut my eyes
When I open them I say *Haha Death—you didn't get me this time*

I've nothing better to do than talk about why diagonally cut toast
is so much better than toast that's cut straight through the middle

Houdini had it figured out
except he kept getting out of the chains

Escape is a six-letter word like heroin
but all the spoons in my house are dirty

and I don't feel like turning on the dishwasher
—the stack of dishes is proof I exist

I listen to the radio all day waiting
just to hear the Dj say *Up next—10 piles of shit in a row*

If I were a telemarketer
I would call my own house and ask to speak to myself

The voice of our generation is still sleeping
Can you call back later?

I call back later
I get the same reply

Good things come to those that don't move
I should be in heaven

Just ask the couch
It's familiar with my backside

Hello Nicor's backside, so good of you to join us
Oh Couch, you know I wouldn't have it any other way

I visit my parents so my mother will give me her love
When she does I yell at her

for giving to me something that precious
because I know she's one person who will no matter what

She says *What's wrong Nicor?*
You seem like such a sad person these days

Not me Ma I'm on cloud six
only three more to go

Before I leave home my mother tells me to be happy
the plane ride is 236 dollars to forget the life below

Up here the clouds carry more weight
I am struggling like a poem

All the ladies with hourglass figures are cracking at the hip
The sand is emptying

The world is lightning
The sun is filling with colors I find I can stare into

I take the American flag to make a blanket from it
and wrap myself in something I remember as once being special

The Mechanics of Geese

Outside the bus is a little rain and a lot of lightning. When the white light cracks across the sky the black night becomes purple. Inside the bus there are no lights on, and it is dark. His head is asleep in her lap, the rest of him follows. His hair is red. Tussled. Like a small boy's mop of unruly hair. He lays breathing gently upon her legs. She sits up in her seat. She has beautiful breasts and lips like cut stone, like folded paper, the crease making petals. Soon she is asleep too, laying across his back as he curves under her like two circles becoming a figure eight, their dreams running into each other. Outside, an eighteen-wheeler zooms by cutting a small patch of light on the damp highway. The trees— they sit like dark lumps. Mouthless gods. If the windows were cleaner the stars might be seen. The boy and girl sleep on. Their bodies curving over one another like the necks of geese, their bodies connecting like some newly discovered 27th letter. They are two trees slowly forming into one. Outside it starts raining more and the machine of hip hop rages on, someplace, somewhere, soundlessly.

THE PLEDGE

Every morning in elementary school
the class would stand with the teacher
raise our left hand, place the right over our heart
and with our principal's voice coming over the PA system
recite the Pledge of Allegiance together.

I pledge allegiance to the flag of the United States of America. And to the republic for which it stands, one nation under God, indivisible, with liberty and justice for all.

And you know the part where it goes
one nation under God, indivisible?

I always thought it was invisible.
And that seemed really cool
because it was like superpowers or something.

One nation under God, invisible

I want my coffin to be painted red white and blue
so in death I am cradled in freedom.

One nation under God, invisible

I want bed sheets
with George Washington and Thomas Jefferson's faces on them
so my forefathers will hold me when I am tired.

One nation under God, invisible

I want the secrets of this country to stop being secrets
and to start being the mistakes we've learned from.
I want my country to be what it once was
to me and a generation of first graders who misheard a word
mistaking our country for one that had superpowers—
a country that could leap buildings in a single bound.
One that carried a green ring
hat manifested the imagination into reality.
One that was a regular guy who still went out into the night
to stop crooks using only his gut his mind and his heart.

One nation under God, indivisible,
with liberty and justice for all—

I used to hear that every morning.
Every morning we had liberty and justice to give to all.

For the 1,680 school time mornings of my childhood
I pledged my allegiance
during the best years of my life
placing my shaking hand over my quaking heart
to make sure it didn't beat its way out of my chest
in the excitement I felt thinking about recess
and chocolate milk on Fridays
and no homework on the weekends
and in being a finger on a hand of fingers
on a hand on an arm of hands
that were the arms of a body of people
who had liberty and justice to give out to every person
who's hearts were beating just as rapidly
as the children standing in Ms. Brown's fourth grade classroom.

In an innocence of kickball and cooties I pledged my allegiance.
And I still pledge my allegiance
to an innocence of kickball and cooties
four square and pigtails and Garbage Pail Kids
and knowing that where I lived was just that:

one nation under God
invisible in its lines and fences
instead of one nation invisible in its presence.

And I know that that nation
is the fire extinguisher on the other side of the glass case
wishing that it was an axe as well
to break itself out.

I know that this country is that heart
beating in the chest of an excited little boy
trying to be patient and learn about the world
pressing his hands over his heart
because he's scared of what may happen if he lifts his palm
and lets his blood sing
because he's scared that being alive means dying
because he's scared to let the red pulsating muscle in his chest
that is no bigger then his fists but so much more
lead him through life.

When I saw *E.T.* for the first time
my mind burned and I was alive.
When I read *The Lion, the Witch, and the Wardrobe*
for the first time
my mind burned and I was alive.
When I danced to Baloo singing "The Bare Necessities"
running round and round my parents' living room
my mind burned and I was alive.
When I was six years old I had all the answers
to all the questions I wasn't asking
and no need for the ones to the ones I was.
When my mind burned and I was alive
I made many pledges to a flap of dyed fabric
holding forgotten colonies and faded stars
that hung limply at the front of the classroom
and I just want a breeze to blow through an open window
and lift it up
so it can start making good on those promises.

FOR A GIRL WHO LIKES THE WORD WOW

snow angels
mud angels
grass angels
pudding angels
water angels
field angels
cloud angels
chiffon angels
taffeta angels
smoke angels
music angels
sand angels
beach angels
street angels
asphalt angels
palm tree angels
car angels
floor angels
mattress angels
skin angels

and God lied down in a big field of it
waving His arms and legs
and laughing loud like it was the first time
and made you

Even If Somebody Pooped a Poem It's Alright Cuz Somebody Somewhere Made It
or
Invincible

I am invincible.
Look at my hands.
These hands are huge.
These hands are big enough to buy somebody a cup of soup.
On good days they can catch bullets as if they were Frisbees.
I am invincible.

I can pick my nose and not care who sees it.
We all have boogers. I know this I do.

I have x-ray vision and I can see that there are boogers in your nose as big and dirty as the ones in mine. So forget me and forget you too for we've all talked crap about people we never knew even though every one of us goes to the bathroom sits down and poos. That's right—miracle of miracles!—I can take food, send it past my teeth and down to my tummy where super power of super powers the food is somehow miraculously transformed into poop! I am invincible! I have a penis! And I can make babies with my penis. Babies that will change into girls and boys who will change into women and men and all that is needed are the super powers known as the vagina and I know that there are people in this world who have these super powers known as the vagina.

I am invincible.

I can close my eyes, fall asleep and see pictures of the sun moving inside my head. When I do, the sun looks fat and flat like a silver dollar too bright to stare at because you can't see all sides of it at the same time but I know that they are there! I know the sun is round, containing volume like a Superball. I know this because I am invincible.

I also know how to make Kool-Aid. Whatever flavor you want.

All that is needed is sugar, water and the power to stir.

I also know what aliens look like: they look like extraterrestrials. I know this because I have seen them. When I draw them. Can you draw them? I ask can you draw them? Not like how I can! I can draw them with green skin and tentacled arms wrapped around red and yellow bubble-shaped ray-guns that can demolish whole buildings in a single shot! And you? You can draw them with robotic bodies and brains inside of glass jars and your aliens are dancing with my aliens and all of our aliens are dancing with each other in the lobby of some space McDonald's somewhere because all spacepeople love French fries, just ask yourself Do I love French fries? Um, YES. Of course you do! Because ALL spacepeople love French fries. Spacepeople live in outer space on spaceplanets and on some spaceplanet a spaceage away spacepeople with green skin and tentacled arms wrapped around red and yellow bubble-shaped ray-pencils are drawing spacepeople with two legs and two arms and hearts inside that go pumppypumpypump and noses that are fat with boogers and lips that are fat like kisses that open and close and open and close and open like poetry—they kiss like poetry, they breathe like poetry, they move like poetry—they poop like poetry! And sometimes they poetry that poop. But even if they poop that poem, that poem is still as strong as a string stuck inside of an ice cube stuck inside an iceberg. We? You and I? We are as unto diamonds. We are diamonds. And I know that sometimes all it takes to be invincible is to know you are such. And I know that you know this too.

Pancakes

I would like to take your heart smoothly out of your breast.
Some nights I can feel it trembling.
Like a quiet train known only by its movement across the midnight rails—
a shiver through a child—
a dog having a dream.
Like a dream inside a leg of mine
I can feel it trembling while you sleep.

I would like to take your heart from out your breast.
And holding it with both hands
gently get up from bed
tip-toe into the kitchen
and place it carefully upon the wooden cutting board

Then pull a rolling pin from its proper drawer
and begin to smooth the heart out
rolling
the pin slowly
tenderly
flattening the soft tissue.

Turn on the radio at a low level
and hum quietly along
my moving arms constant.
I am rowing a boat towards you.

I press down.
Smooth the wrinkles out.
Spread the heart across the cutting boards
until it is flat as a pancake.

Then carefully peel it up
bake it
pour syrup on it
and eat it like one.

The whole thing.

It is a large pancake.
Perfectly cooked.
Sweet and fluffy with a slight crisp to the edge.

I use my fork and knife several times.
It makes many bites.

When it is firmly inside of me
filling up the spaces of me that were not filled
I will wash the utensils the plate the board the pin
and the pan I cooked it in.
I will wash my hands turn off the lights
and head back to bed.
When I climb in you stir a little.
I pull the cover over us
and hold on—
filled with a light so heavy
it is the color of gold.

And you
are finally calm.
Filled with a space so wide and dark
that the silence in you becomes something soft.
The night spreads itself like ink
noiselessly inside of you
adjusting ever so slightly your wet stars
that they float down quietly to lie in our bed
and calmly fall asleep beside you.

I'm Forgetting This Poem Before I Write It

trying to write this
while crossing 23rd street
en route to the subway
my watch gets in the way

my watch and women!

boarding the train
I see a girl that looks like pink lemonade
pink lemonade with ice!

then the rest of the picnic comes in

the rest of the picnic
and the ants
and the bugs that eat the ants
and all the people who step on bugs and ants

this train car got crowded quick
where's that pink lemonade

between shoulders like bookends
I can barely feel the blessing of the 6 train's air-conditioning
it feels like the number 2

the doors shut
and the bell of their closing
sounds like *thank you*
or *fuck you*
depending
on the mood

the train doesn't move
we stand awkwardly
all waiting
for a fireworks show to happen
underground
passengers standing
like relatives at a reunion who only have blood in common

I wonder what would be their reaction
if I were to start a sing-a-long

the train throws itself forward
I hold on
to nothing
and balance
like all this was a surfboard
my muscles are stronger than I think

I bob my head to my headphones
like an egg in the ocean
following the flow of the train's
for the length of the ride
we dance
it leads

at my stop I come out
from under the ground
and smile in the warm light

the word liberty is six feet long
on the back of a garbage truck

beautiful women like bodegas
on every corner

my arms are overcoats thrown off of the Sears Tower
my arms are bow ties that spin

I am filled with a kind wildness

later when writing this
I wished I could remember
what this poem was about

but while still on the street
I pass a trash heap and stop to face it
I let the heat from my body burn the trash like an x-ray
and the fever in me burns its silhouette into the cardboard
the shape looks the definition of definition
I stand there while the fire of the setting sun
ignites everything else in the city

THE STORY OF ICARUS

The wings
were tired of moving.
So he sat down on a bench in the park
with the other young cats.
And sitting in the collective thoughts
of loneliness and cigarettes
he folded his wings
burned them
and bummed a smoke.
I watched it all from my window.

The Branches Are Full & the Orchards Heavy

Gentlemen have you forgotten your God?
He weeps out loud
waiting for our dreams to grow like ears
while you are making ghosts out of people.
You are making ghosts from your Torah,
your Koran, your Bibles.

We have shaved our books down,
swallowed them
so that the word of God
might flow through us.
But the pages just sit in our bellies,
speaking to us in dull murmurs as we sleep.
We wonder *What do I do?*
Make me understand.
We wish to become one with our Lord.
We hear the voices and think we know what they say
This is the word of God—
I hear this—
I heard this correctly!
So we rise and try to translate this word
through the work, through the hearts.
We search through beds
between thighs
between the blanket the leg
the needle twist fuck and the fuck you curse of the moon
to find our Lord and listen more proper-like.
But our ears are too small
for our hearts to understand the humming
of these sentences singing inside of us.

We are trying to decipher the bang buck braille
of Your silent throat Lord,

but the voices grow and grow fuzzy still.
So we stand and go to the kitchen
and pick up knives to cut these voices out from inside.
We stab ourselves
—I must hear you—
cutting the flap of skin

the words twist on the floor of our homes
mixing their sounds with our blood.
They drown
but it does not stop—
I must hear You
—we hear the same songs
singing in the stomachs of others.
So we grab more knives to cut those out
but there are more and more stomachs—
we need bigger knives. We need soldiers
tanks and missiles but we still cannot make out the words.
We need dead mothers and children raped from searching.
The hospitals are full and overflowing
from our trying to cut our God from our gut
with the blade the pipe
the fingernail twist of the drug
pushed and poked through the arm to the belly
to throw Him up.
In the bang of the scream
we find our savior—
the shell in the chamber
is a quiet plea to a distant God
asking for us to be remembered by Him—
through the tire tread
through the smoke of the tank
the crunch of the skull
through the babies we bury beneath us—
we empty their tiny limbs to see
if a scrap of our Lord still lingers somewhere inside there.
We clutch throats pistols and palms
in the same two handed clasp of prayer
staring into the mirror we see crypts
fondling the marble of our hearts like they were mausoleums
we are ghosts—
hungry for something bigger
than what our mouths are kissing.
Let me see You Lord!
Let me see You.

See me balancing myself
in the middle of the question.
Black as my eye

beaten by Your hymn,
I am holding still.

So go ahead.
You gentle
men of God.
You tender sinners.
Take your rifles
raise to my gut and fire on.
Hear the song more clearly—
it does not sing what you wish it did
It is too big for us to see even a letter of it
so do not even try. Instead
cut Him from me.
I wish to drape His face with my kisses
and finally sleep softly.

CRADLE

Set the warriors to sea in a ship stacked with shields, layers of swords, mountains of gold. Lay them out with their wives. With their children. Lay them out with their livestock, with the whole farm. The rain is not coming here. Not today. For today the gods welcome one of their own back home. So set the hero out on the soft waves that will carry him to the other side of the pink ether where he will float on fire until the ash consumes him like the mighty warrior he once was and like the legend he will become. The flames will dance over his possessions, his goblets and arrows, his blankets, his paintings, his passions. The flames will dance across his flesh like the soft fingers of the soft lover he left, and as he sleeps this last sleep, the fires will eat him away, the heat will write his skin across the night sky to join the constellations that will guide the sailors at storm, the herders lost in the clouds. They will all come home by facing the direction his eyes are facing. The heavens are filled with smoke. This is history this is legend this is what we once were. Where the stories come from, what we are. When you fall in battle, they will take your body with the life you made in this world and set it off to sail behind you into the next, so that you will stay a king, remain forever the golden being you breathed as on this side of the mountain. When you pass, may your life follow you like a shadow into the light. When I go, bury me with nothing but my own skin. I spent far too many days trying to outrun this thing called mine, so if I set myself into your arms would you hold me like the earth, quietly? I am yours. Give me a field, give me a big sky. A mountain. Give me your mouth. I'm just looking for a quiet place that I could die inside of.

Almond Milk & Tilapia

What they don't tell you about getting married is the mess.
That the gifts come early.
And you end up too busy
to stack the shambles
the house is becoming.
All week the floor has been a poor man's library.
Today I put most of the books away.
The first editions on the top shelf.
The paperbacks just below. Steinbeck's Penguins
spines of orange.
After that I organized the desk and moved her piano.
Moved the gold couch that traveled with me from Oregon.
Vacuumed the living room.
Sat down. Watched a moment.
The moment moved like a small fish.
Or a slow satellite.
I took the folded clothes from the hamper
and put them in the dresser. Finally.
Hung up her dress with the whales on it.
Made sure the hangers all turned the same direction
and left for the grocery store.
Went by way of the tall grass.
All this cement. It wishes
for something else in itself.
The super market is a temple of air conditioning.
Picked up almond milk and fish. The doors sing when they move.
Got dizzy on the walk back and drank water when I got home.
I need to visit the eye doctor.
I made a quiet sandwich for lunch.
Ate in the living room of our tiny house
before opening the world again.
It is hard work being a poet.
All this daylight one must contend with.
Right now I am sitting at the coffeeshop down the street.
Tried writing four poems. They have not been easy.
They are a rusting bicycle. I am a sleepy boxer.
In the afternoon my left is unfocused. My tea sits
untouched, its ice all melted. I stare at the computer,
a contest of two concrete ships racing.

I ended up in court with a Chinese drunkard.
Fell into the water from his boat
and laughed into the hole of the snowy moon.
An iceberg drifts across the sky
returning the present to me.
The air in here is heavy and hot
could grow vines inside itself.
My tongue is dry.
So is my pen. There is a well
somewhere over the hill. All the dance
is a different country from where I sit.
I want my pockets to burn
but they only buzz.
She calls,
tells me she is on her way home
and will meet me here shortly.
In May I will have tiny flowers pinned to my breast
and she a peacock feather in her hair.
What glorious sounds the sun shall make.
Here my wife-to-be has just walked through the door,
dancing her way into my periphery.
I think of the tilapia in the refrigerator.
When we go home we will cook it
and have bread.

How a Person Finds Home

When you are walking down the street in some city that is not
the one you come from

with the sun in your eyes so perhaps you are squinting or
perhaps because of how brightly everything shines

you have tears falling out and you find you cannot look directly
at the world before you

and there is a song from an open window that resembles
the birthday pocketknife you received at ten

and the 16th note is a bridge bending over cold stones
that your brother walks upon

and those cold stones sing a sound similar to your name
similar to library brick similar to porch swing and tea cup

similar to your grandmother's name and your arms feel like her
loose but smooth skin

and your face remembers your grandfather's rough cheeks
the smell of his aftershave

and as you are pulled in the direction of where you come from
you will see a suit with no one in it

running from far off in the distance and this body-less suit
is running directly towards you

a hundred people moving in the streets but the suit
is running to you

and you can not move away or towards it any faster or slower
than how you are already moving

and the suit will come up to you and without body or lung
will be breathing hard

and without skull or mouth will ask if you have the time and you
without watch or clock will say

Yes I do and as you lift your wrist you hear the suit without hands
or throat lift his palms and whisper between them

"Will you unbutton these jackets of mine? Will you pull me on
and button the buttons in my vest back up?"

And when you do the vest will feel like a coffin that does not
need to wait for death to be slept in

but instead is simply a lidless boat for the grass to grow through
for the daylight to touch itself upon

for the dark and the stars to fall towards and fill and all around
you the night will rise like a river over the city

while you sit in the middle of its waters running your hands over
your belly rubbing fabric between your fingers thinking

"These are the softest clothes I've ever felt."
This is the closest thing I can draw to a map.

With you on one end and me on the other
and no space between.

HARVESTING MELONS

My heart is made of white stone
and is tall
you made this
with your hands
you pulled the stones
from the mud yourself
and stacked them on the river's bank
one atop the other
the honey dew melons
full on the vines
watching
you stood back
hands dripping
wiped across your legs
stared at it
marveling in the sunlight
at how easy it was to do this
how much the rocks wanted
to be something
that your fingers pushed together
that they almost floated
inside your palms
and sung to be lifted into the air

SHAKE THE DUST

This is for the fat girls.

This is for the little brothers.

This is for the schoolyard wimps and for the childhood bullies who tormented them. For the former prom queen and for the milk crate ballplayers. For the nighttime cereal eaters and for the retired elderly Wal-Mart store front door greeters.

Shake the dust.

This is for the benches and the people sitting upon them.

For the bus drivers driving a million broken hymns. For the men who have to hold down three jobs simply to hold up their children for the night schoolers and for the midnight bike riders trying to fly.

Shake the dust.

For the 2-year-olds who cannot be understood because they speak half-English and half-God. Shake the dust.

For the boys with the beautiful sisters.

Shake the dust.

For the girls with the brothers who are going crazy, for those gym class wallflowers, for the 12-year-olds afraid of taking public showers. For the kid who's always late to class because he forgets the combination to his locker, for the girl who loves somebody else. Shake the dust.

This is for the hard men who want love but know that it won't come. For the ones who are forgotten. The ones the amendments do not stand up for. For the ones who are told speak only when you are spoken to and then are never spoken to. Speak every time you stand, so you do not forget yourself. Do not let a moment go by that doesn't remind you that your heart beats thousands of times every day and that there are enough gallons of blood to make every one of us oceans. Do not settle for letting these waves settle and for the dust to collect in your veins.

This is for the celibate pedophile who keeps on struggling. For the poetry teachers and for the people who go on vacations alone. For the sweat that drips off of Mick Jagger's singing lips. For the shaking skirt on Tina Turner's shaking hips. For the heavens and for the hells through which Tina has lived.

This is for the tired and for the dreamers.
For the families that will never be like the Cleavers,
with perfectly made dinners and sons like Wally and the Beaver.
This is for the bigots, for the sexists, for the killers, for the big house pen-sentenced cats becoming redeemers, and for the springtime that always seems to know to show up after every one of our winters.

This is for you.

Make sure that by the time the fisherman returns you are gone. Because just like the days, I burn at both ends and every time I write, every time I open my eyes, I am cutting out parts of myself just to give them to you. So shake the dust. And take me with you when you do. For none of this has ever been for me. All that pushes and pulls, it pushes for you.

So grab this world by its clothespins, and shake it out
again and again.
And hop on top
and take it for a spin.
And when you hop off,
shake it again.
For this is yours.
Make these words worth it.
Make this not just another poem that I write.

Not just another poem like just another night, that sits heavy above us all. Walk into it, breath it in. Let it crawl though the halls of your arms, like the millions of years of millions of poets coursing like blood, pumping and pushing, making you live, shaking the dust. So when the world knocks at your door, clutch the knob tightly and open on up. And run forward. Run forward as fast and as far as you must. Run into its widespread greeting arms with your hands outstretched before you, fingertips trembling though they may be.

ABOUT THE AUTHOR

Anis Mojgani is a two-time National Poetry Slam Champion and winner of the International World Cup Poetry Slam. His work has appeared on HBO and NPR. A TEDx Speaker and former resident of the Oregon Literary Arts Writers-In-The-Schools program, Anis has performed for audiences as varied as those of the House of Blues and the United Nations. Anis is also the author of two other poetry collections, both published by Write Bloody: *Over the Anvil We Stretch* (2008) and *The Feather Room* (2011). Originally from New Orleans, he currently lives in Austin, TX in a little house with his wife and their dog Trudy.

ACKNOWLEDGEMENTS

Some of these poems first appeared in the poetry chapbooks I self published between 2001 and 2005: *Where Are You Moon?!*, *The Ballad of Nicor Misgoni*, *Untitled*, and *The Birthday Yard*. Certain poems first appeared in *Rattle, Used Furniture Review, Muzzle Magazine, The Legendary, Bestiary, Union Station*, the three volumes of The Poetry Revival anthologies, and *Spoken Word Revolution Redux*.

The actual and full title of the poem "On the day his son was born, the astronomer screamed out the window" is "On the day his son was born, the astronomer screamed out the window, 'You! This! This thing that beats the inside of our hearts? Is a beautiful curse! Know this & fling it hard enough into the air to make new charts!' Shortly afterwards, the astronomer realized his newborn son, his wife, & the birth all were but hallucinations, so he sat with a pot of tea & became a trapeze artist instead." But was edited down for the sake of formatting.

The phrase "kind wildness" from "I'm forgetting this poem..." was flipped from the song "The Wild Kindness" by Silver Jews.

Thank you to Mr. Brown, Ms. O'Keffe Aptowicz, and Mrs. Mojgani for your help with the editing of this book. To weave together a bunch of disparate poems that span 15 years was at times a frustrating task. Thank you for your feedback and for realigning my focus when it wavered.

It is an honor and blessing to be a part of Write Bloody and its journey. So thank you again, Derrick, for all the work you put into this press. It is a work of miraculous magic.

And thank you, Alexis. I am thankful to be your husband. Everyday and always. I love you. Everyday and always.

If You Like Anis Mojgani,
Anis Mojgani Likes...

The New Clean
Jon Sands

Slow Dance with Sasquatch
Jeremy Radin

Racing Hummingbirds
Jeanann Verlee

I Love Science!
Shanny Jean Maney

Everything Is Everything
Cristin O'Keefe Aptowicz

Write Bloody Publishing distributes and promotes great books of fiction, poetry and art every year. We are an independent press dedicated to quality literature and book design, with an office in Austin, TX.

Our employees are authors and artists so we call ourselves a family. Our design team comes from all over America: modern painters, photographers and rock album designers create book covers we're proud to be judged by.

We publish and promote 8-12 tour-savvy authors per year. We are grass-roots, D.I.Y., bootstrap believers. Pull up a good book and join the family. Support independent authors, artists and presses.

**Want to know more about Write Bloody books, authors and events?
Join our maling list at**

www.writebloody.com

WRITEBLOODY
QUALITY AMERICAN BOOKS

WRITE BLOODY BOOKS

1,000 Black Umbrellas — Daniel McGinn

38 Bar Blues — C.R. Avery

After the Witch Hunt — Megan Falley

Aim for the Head, Zombie Anthology — Robbie Q. Telfer, editor

American Buckeye — Shappy Seasholtz

Amulet — Jason Bayani

Animal Ballistics — Sarah Morgan

Any Psalm You Want — Khary Jackson

Birthday Girl with Possum — Brendan Constantine

The Bones Below — Sierra deMulder

Born in the Year of the Butterfly Knife — Derrick C. Brown

Bring Down the Chandeliers — Tara Hardy

Ceremony for the Choking Ghost — Karen Finneyfrock

City of Insomnia — Victor D. Infante

The Constant Velocity of Trains — Lea C. Deschenes

Courage: Daring Poems for Gutsy Girls — Karen Finneyfrock, Mindy Nettifee
& Rachel McKibbens, Editors

Dear Future Boyfriend — Cristin O'Keefe Aptowicz

Don't Smell the Floss — Matty Byloos

Drunks and Other Poems of Recovery — John X.

The Elephant Engine High Dive Revival anthology

Everything is Everything — Cristin O'Keefe Aptowicz

The Feather Room — Anis Mojgani

Gentleman Practice — Buddy Wakefield

Glitter in the Blood: A Guide to Braver Writing — Mindy Nettifee

Good Grief — Stevie Smith

The Good Things About America — Derrick Brown and Kevin Staniec, Editors

Great Balls of Flowers — Steve Abee

Hot Teen Slut — Cristin O'Keefe Aptowicz

Henhouse: The International Book for Chickens & Their Lovers — Buddy Wakefield

How to Seduce a White Boy in Ten Easy Steps — Laura Yes Yes